www.thetalented10th.net

All rights reserved, including the right to reproduce this book or portions thereof in any form whatsoever. For information address The Talented 10th: 7806 S Harvard Blvd Los Angeles CA, 90047

Copyright © 2016 by Ashley Feazell

Paperback edition 2016

For information about special discounts for bulk purchases, please contact ashley@thetalented10th.net or call 323-395-3787

ISBN 978-0-9994620-

INDEX

Pg. 1 Introduction
Pg. 2 Brenda Marsh-Mitchell
Pg. 3 Danny J. Bakewell Sr.
Pg. 4 Lillian Mobley
Pg. 5 Dr. George McKenna
Pg. 6 Maulana Karenga
Pg. 7 Yvonne Wheeler
Pg. 8 Mary Henry
Pg. 9 Nipsey Hussle
Pg. 10 Johnnie Tillmon
Pg. 11 John W. Mack

Introduction

Everyone is special. We all have certain things we can do better than others. This is our talent, and it is our responsibility to acknowledge it, and use it for good. In the Talented Tenth: Historical and Present, we will acknowledge and highlight the achievements', and talents of our culture's historical and present figures. These books will explore the vast Pan-African community and focus on its greatness. Each book will focus on 10 specific figures.

In this book The Talented Tenth: Historical and Present, one will discover Community Leaders of Los Angeles. These 10 figures have worked tirelessly to improve the community they call home, Los Angeles. Through hard work and determination these figures have improved the quality of living for the community they inhabit. They are the leaders that walk and live amongst the people. Through protesting, enterprising, organizing, teaching and building these figures have not only become community legends but national treasures.

Brenda Marsh-Mitchell

1947-2014

Brenda Marsh-Mitchell was born and raised in Los Angeles, California. She was born in 1947 and attended Vermont Avenue, 24th street Elementary, Foshay Middle School, and Betsy Ross for High School. As a youngster she enjoyed the lively events of the infamous Central Avenue and witnessed the glorious pride of a thriving black community. She worked many jobs before becoming an employee of the Brotherhood Crusade and The Bakewell Companies.

Marsh-Mitchell became essential to the organization as Director of Governmental Affairs, eventually becoming the right hand to its then president, Danny Bakewell Sr. She credited Bakewell with teaching her how to respect her community and always be of service. She was not only an integral part of Brotherhood Crusade, but a vital community mentor. She organized voter registrations, created programs to help feed the homeless, helped mobilize thousands of participants for the Million Man March, created community job placement events but her biggest accomplishment is being founding president of Mothers In Action. "Taste of Soul" is a street festival created by Danny Bakewell, that helps small community businesses thrive, and families unite. Vendors line up on a shut-down Crenshaw Boulevard, people shop, eat and party to live music. Marsh-Mitchell helped her boss grow the events attendance over 10x and the event is a staple within the city of Los Angeles. Mothers In Action is a non-profit organization created to improve the quality of life for the community's children, families and overall well-being. She founded the organization in 1992 and built its membership five-thousand strong. Joining forces with instrumental women like Lillian Mobley and Johnnie Tillmon helped the organization take on overlooked community concerns such as police brutality, welfare, health, senior citizens and education. In her own words "Every morning when I wake up, I say lord let me help change the quality of life for somebody", and everyday of her life she blessed her community with acts of kindness that would shape the Los Angeles district. In 2014 Los Angeles lost an earthly angel when Marsh-Mitchell passed away.

Brenda Marsh-Mitchell was a staple in her community. One has not done business in Los Angeles without crossing her path. She has worked with dignitaries, politicians, community leaders, entertainers, church leaders, CEO's and the list goes on. Her helpful spirit was passed to her three daughters and two grandsons, who continue her legacy of service. A giving soul and humble servant Brenda Marsh-Mitchell was a Los Angeles mentor encouraging the youth to "Take your time and do the work".

Danny J. Bakewell Sr.
1946

Danny Joseph Bakewell was born October 17, 1946, in New Orleans Louisiana. He graduated St. Augustine High School and married his high school sweetheart Aline. They conceived a son Danny Jr., the event prompted Bakewell to move to California for better opportunities to provide for his family.

Moving to Los Angeles in 1968 proved to be the best decision for the Bakewell Family. The couple had two more children and Danny Sr. found employment as a community organizer, and Director of Careers at the University of California, Los Angeles, before becoming president and CEO of Brotherhood Crusade. The organization is one of Bakewell's biggest accomplishments growing an organization that helps people that are strategically misinformed and mistreated. Establishing the Brotherhood Crusade has raised millions of dollars for community initiatives targeting senior citizens, domestic violence, jail reform, mentorship, health, nutrition, education, voter registration and much more. In 1982 Bakewell became CEO of The Bakewell Company which has become one of the largest black development companies in the nation. Working tirelessly to give back and build his community, he purchased New Orleans radio station WBOK and *The Los Angeles Sentinel*, two media outlets that glorify and highlight the achievements of its people. Consistently battling with community injustices, Bakewell became one of the leading voices of criticism of the ruling in the Latasha Harlins case. He is the creator of the infamous Los Angeles Taste of Soul. A festival created to encourage economics and amplify the culture of his community. The festival has become a staple of the community, annually shutting down Crenshaw boulevard to give community businesses opportunities to grow economically. A community mentor, he has been honored with numerous awards for his service, including a school named after him located in Los Angeles, the Danny J. Bakewell Primary Center.

Bakewell's activism and philanthropy have positively affected Los Angeles in tremendous ways, he and his wife founded "Sabriya's Castle of Fun", in honor of their youngest daughter that lost her life to Leukemia. The foundation has established hospital programs around the country aimed to aid young children in their battle with life threatening diseases. His humble spirit allows him to mentor and council masses. An obscure leader and brother amongst the people. Danny Bakewell Sr. the consummate businessman and boss, a modern-day nobleman.

Lillian Mobley

1930-2011

Lillian Mobley was born Lillian Harkness March 29, 1930 in Macon, Georgia. She graduated from high school in 1948 and shortly after married. Mobley moved to Los Angeles in 1951 with husband James Otis Mobley, they had four children. She united with activists Mary Henry and Johnnie Tillmon to advocate for the building of the Charles Drew/Martin Luther king Medical Center and was a key member fighting to keep it open after Henry's death. A champion for healthcare, seniors, and education for the underprivileged. She was instrumental in the creation of King Drew Magnet High School of Medicine, where a bronzed bust is displayed in her honor. In 1980 she was elected delegate to the Democratic National Convention. She organized several food and clothing giveaways and became executive director of the South-Central Multipurpose Senior Citizen Center in 1983 renamed, The Lillian Mobley Center. She has served on countless boards in fields that are commonly overlooked. Her passion to serve her community creates a spotlight that draws attention to her contagious, warm, caring spirit. Mobley became vital in not only highlighting the everyday struggles of the local community but instrumental in the repairing of the issues.
An instrumental figure concerning the well-being of the underprivileged after the 1992 riots of Los Angeles. A true voice of the people, her work is captured in the 1994 documentary "The Fire This Time". A quiet person with a huge presence Mobley's spirit could move a crowd. In her own words she, "enjoyed fighting for the rights of others." Lillian Mobley the people's advocate.

Dr. George McKenna

1940

George J. McKenna III was born September 6, 1940 in New Orleans, Louisiana. Born to educated parents, the eldest of three boys, his mother a middle school principal and father a dean. Education was paramount for McKenna growing up, both of his parents received degrees from Xavier. He graduated from Xavier with a Bachelor's degree in Mathematics. He also earned his Master's in Mathematics from Loyola University and holds a Doctor of Education from Xavier University. In 1962, he moved to California to work with the Los Angeles Unified School District while attending Loyola Law School. In 1979 McKenna followed in his parents' footsteps and became principal of Washington Preparatory High School. The school, gang infested with few literate scholars, leaving McKenna to work with a disorganized, ancient, broken system. Going above and beyond the principal job, McKenna went into the neighborhood knocking on doors to recruit and assure children of Washington's ability to get scholars into college. His reforms changed the school atmosphere with no graduates, to one with 80% of graduates going to college. Washington Preparatory High School's turn around recognized nationally with McKenna being recruited by school and police districts to advise on reformation. McKenna was played by Denzel Washington in "The George McKenna Story", which aired on CBS and became an award-winning movie.

George McKenna is a grassroots organizer using his educational background to elevate the poor circumstances of an inner-city high school. He is currently a LAUSD board member and has received over 400 award, including his election to the National Alliance of Black School Educators' Hall of Fame and the Congressional Black Caucus' Chairman's Award. George McKenna a radical reformer, repairing educational dilemmas for the future of his community.

Maulana Karenga

1941

Maulana Karenga was born Ronald McKinley Everett July 14, 1941, in Parsonburg Maryland. His father was a tenant farmer and a minister. Coming from a sharecropping family Karenga was no stranger to hard work.

He moved to Los Angeles in 1955 joining his older brother and attended Los Angeles City College. He became the first black student president at LACC. He earned a bachelor's degree from University of California Los Angeles and during this time changed his name which means master teacher, keeper of tradition. Karenga became a founding member of the political activist group US, which was formed from the aftermath of the Watts Riots. The group US had ideological and fundamental differences with the Los Angeles chapter of the Black Panthers and violent arguments often ensued even though both groups were fighting for black empowerment. The two group's entanglements eventually caused the deaths of Black Panther members. Like many civil rights leaders he believed to be constantly spied upon by governmental agencies, which created extreme paranoia. Maulana Karenga was imprisoned on charges of false imprisonment, and felony assault in 1971 and paroled in 1975. US disbanded while Karenga was in prison and he maintains his innocence believing himself to have been a political prisoner. These setbacks didn't deter his support to educate black people on their true heritage. Karenga is the creator of Kwanzaa, a celebration of African heritage created to connect African Americans with their African roots. It is celebrated annually December 26 through January 1. He is the author of seventeen books and hold two PHD's both with concentrations in African affairs. He has become one of the leading voices of Maatian ethical thought, an interpretation on Egyptology as it relates to African heritage. He has created tons of organizations to help shape the black political and intellectual culture. A professor and chair of the department of Africana Studies at California State University, Long Beach. His extensive study and life experiences make him a leading voice in Africana studies as he travels the world lecturing on the subject. Maulana Karenga has received countless awards for his service to the community, activism, and intellectual achievements. A living historical figure aiming to create a new future by cultivating young minds to understand their true heritage. Maulana Karenga a 21st century revolutionary.

Yvonne Wheeler
1958

Yvonne Wheeler was born May 13, 1958 in Baton Rouge, Louisiana. The daughter of a Baton Rouge union activist she was familiar with activism and used direct action at a young age to produce favorable results. In 1965 she was able to attend a desegregated high school, but the school failed to provide school buses for transportation. Wheeler and a group of students marched to the district offices. Arrest were made but the students received school buses to transport them to school. She attended Southern University, became married and worked at South Central Bell until 1984.

Laid off from her job at South Central Bell and separated from her husband Wheeler needed a fresh start so in 1991 she moved to Los Angeles. She challenged authority when a complaint about a rude black operator led to all the black operators being disciplined. The reprimand was unfair because history of rudeness was a factor, only blackness. This led to Wheeler being elected a member of the union executive board and steward. She was elected local union vice-president from 1996-1999 fearlessly challenging questionable managerial practices and rules. Breaking down bearers while facing sexism and racism, she became president of the Los Angeles Chapter in 1996. The same year she became president of the California State A. Philip Randolph Institute, an organization focusing on integrating the African American community with the labor movement. The paired positions allowed Wheeler to become a leader in the community mentoring African Americans into the workforce. Her focus to help African Americans gain leadership position within labor unions. She was able to defeat Gov. Pete Wilson's anti-labor proposition with the help of Brenda Marsh-Mitchell and her network of community leaders. They were able to gather the black vote to defeat prop 226 which was designed to bust up labor unions. In 1999, Wheeler became the first African –American elected president of the Communications Workers of American Local 9586, winning numerous awards. The work she did with mentor Marsh-Mitchell inspired her to continue to give back and mentor others. She was recruited to be a national representative by the AFL-CIO and became lead representative in 2003. She helped the AFL-CIO campaign for Obama in 2008 and Clinton in 2016. She was the lead AFL-CIO organizer for the first annual International Human Rights Day.

Yvonne Wheeler is the masked hero living amongst the people. She is the woman behind major strikes like the longshore union lockout and supermarket strike, she stopped Arnold Schwarzenegger's special election in 2005. The traditional activist, her methods are straight forward and involve organizing the community. Any hurdles she faced seemed to fuel not only her personal ascension, but her passion to keep others from facing the same problems. Yvonne Wheeler the Los Angeles contender.

Mary Henry
1926-2009

Mary Henry was born Mary Elizabeth Bradshaw August 7, 1926 in Cedartown, Georgia but grew up in Gary, Indiana and witnessed the power of community. Henry moved to Los Angeles with husband Louis Charles Henry in 1957 to seek better opportunities for their family, they had four sons. When she arrived, she carried the same community values she enjoyed in Indiana, along with her to Los Angeles. Her presence in Los Angeles not only bettered her family's future but bettered the community. Joining forces with other like-minded women like Johnnie Tillmon and Lillian Mobley helped create an immovable network that mended a community. She served as the Avalon –Carver Community Center director for 30 years. Mary Henry helped to establish Charles Drew/Martin Luther King Medical Center, after the Watts Riots. She served on Lyndon B. Johnson's War on Poverty task force and helped to create the Head Start Program. She also served as member and president of the Compton Unified School District Board of Trustees. *The Los Angeles Times* woman of the year in 1967. Her work honored by magazines, newspapers, governors and presidents for her community service. She tirelessly worked to create a better future for the generations to come.

Henry is described as the fabric of the community as she worked to make a change from within its borders and became the glue that put things back together after both Los Angeles riots. A mentor to many Los Angeles community leaders Maxine Waters being one of them, she prided herself on nurturing the young mind of a future leader and seeing them live up to their expectations as leaders of the community. Mary Henry a neighborhood titan that helped mold future community pilots.

Nipsey Hussle
1985-2019

Nipsey Hussle was born Ermias Ashgedom August 15, 1985 in Los Angeles, California. Born to and African American mother and Eritrean father the middle child of three children. He grew up in Los Angeles in the 90's which was afflicted by gangs, drugs and police brutality. He attended Open School Elementary, Audubon Middle School and Hamilton High School. Hussle dropped out of high school and left home, drawn to the afflictions of his community. At the age of 19 he and his eldest brother traveled with his father to Eritrea, which became a life changing trip. The pilgrimage changed Hussle's outlook on life and the importance of community and self sufficiency. Upon his return to the United States of America he became serious about rapping and released a mix tape in 2005 *Slauson Boy Volume 1* the underground success allowed for the budding artist to put out another mix tape and sign to Cinematic Group and Epic records. He continued to garner underground success releasing mixtapes and taking small acting jobs and in 2008 he became a father. The birth of his daughter created an increasing passion for success, which he eventually achieved after leaving Epic. Gaining breakout attention in 2010 with mixtape *The Marathon* and featured as a freshman on the cover of rap magazine *XXL*. He released a follow up mixtape, *The Marathon Continues* in 2011. His music captured the essence of the Los Angeles streets. He also began his journey to self sufficiency opening small businesses to help generate community jobs and wealth. In 2013 he released mixtape *Crenshaw*, with 1000 limited edition copies sold for $100 a copy, an advancement in traditional marketing. He released mixtapes almost yearly and in 2016 also became a father for the second time. In 2017 he opened The Marathon Clothing Store, in his community. An advocate for self-sufficiency he often spoke out about community deficiencies and offered educational resources to help his neighborhood. In 2018 Nipscy Hussle released his studio album *Victory Lap* it debut on the billboard charts at number four, the race seemed to have been won but unfortunately in 2019 he was assassinated in front of his store in his community.

Nipsey Hussle was an innovative entrepreneur and gifted story-teller. A champion of the streets turning his passion into a lucrative career. His remarkable work ethic became apart of his name. Encompassing the strength of iron to continue his pursuit of success which prompted his motto "The Marathon". Nipsey Hussle the mighty soldier and vanguard of Los Angeles.

Johnnie Tillmon

1926-1995

Johnnie Tillmon was born April 10, 1926 in Scott, Arkansas. The daughter of a migrant sharecropper. She joined her brothers in California in 1959 and worked as a shop steward in a Compton laundry. She organized workers and became involved in the Nickerson Garden Planning Organization, an organization created to improve the housing project living conditions.

Tillmon became ill and was forced to go on welfare. She experienced the harsh treatment of the harassing welfare caseworkers. During this time caseworkers would go into a recipients' house and try to find evidence of extra income. The turbulent life of a single mother on welfare was depicted in the movie "Claudine". In 1963, Tillmon organized the residents of the housing projects and formed ANC Mothers Anonymous. The group, made up of welfare mothers, concentrated on solving the problems they faced while handling affairs with the system. The group became apart of the national welfare recipient organization, National Welfare Rights Organization and Tillmon became chairman. In 1972, she published an article in *Ms Magazine*, "Welfare is a Woman's Issue". The article highlighted the unfair treatment of women on welfare and how the government purposely or inadvertently controlled the lives of women on welfare. The NWRO organized welfare recipients but the board that controlled the organization were made up of men that had never been on welfare. Tillmon challenged the governing board and won but the organizations funds had been depleted.

Johnnie Tillmon was a strong, independent mother turned activist. She saw the need for change and became the voice of the voiceless. Strongly believing in fair treatment for all, she continued her fight to correct any injustice inflicted upon the less fortunate. Her strong, relentless demeanor helped push forward correcting initiatives that helped her community. Johnnie Tillmon the radical mother of Los Angeles.

John W. Mack
1937-2018

John Wesley Mack was born January 6, 1937 in Kingstree, South Carolina but his family moved to Darlington, South Carolina shortly after his birth. His mother a school-teacher and his father a minister. He graduated high school and attended North Carolina A&T State University and in 1958 he earned a B.S. in applied sociology.

Mack married Harriet Johnson and they had three children. He earned a Master's degree from Clark Atlanta and co-founded the Commission on Appeal for Human Rights. This organization integrated students from Morehouse, Spelman and Atlanta University to stage sit-ins and conduct peaceful protest for human civil rights. Mack's mentor Whitney Young sent Mack to California for a social work fellowship at Camarillo Hospital which was completed in 1964. In 1965 he became the Executive Director of the Flint, Michigan Urban League focusing on fair housing and voter registration. Mack became president of the Los Angeles Urban League in 1969 and produced one of the country's most prosperous non-profit organization, focusing on economic development, education and employment. The organization, under Mack's leadership procured an annual $25 million dollar budget.

While serving as president for Los Angeles Urban League he also co-founded the Los Angeles Black Leadership Coalition on Education and appointed to other positions such as vice president of the United Way Corporation of Council Executives and Fellowship in Residence at Harvard University. He retired from his position at Los Angeles Urban league in 2005 after serving the longest tenure ever held in the president position. The same year, Mack was appointed President of the Board of Police Commissioners of Los Angeles where he would serve as either President or Vice-President until 2014. An activist at heart, he fought for reforms to change the overall culture of the LAPD concerning bias policing. John Mack Elementary School, located near USC is a vibrant elementary school in the heart of Los Angeles.

John Mack was a leader amongst the people during the civil rights movement. He carried with him to Los Angeles his beliefs, policies and means to achieve community well-being. Honored by the Los Angeles Business Journal as one of 500 most influential leaders in Los Angeles in 2016, his legacy is deep-rooted in the city. John W. Mack an incomparable executive and activist of Los Angeles.

1. Mary Henry help establish which Los Angeles staple?

a. Drew/MLK medical center

b. Watts youth center

c. Jesse Owens park

2. Dr. George McKenna revived which Los Angeles high school?

a. Crenshaw High

b. Washington Prep

c. Dorsey High

3. Which Los Angeles organization did Brenda Marsh-Mitchell become founding president?

a. Taste of Soul

b. Mothers In Action

c. Brotherhood Crusade

4. As the chairman of this foundation John W. Mack kept which organization's yearly revenue at 25 million?

a. Brotherhood Crusade

b. NAACP

c. Los Angeles Urban League

5. Johnnie Tillmon organized the residents of which housing project?

a. Nickerson garden

b. Willmington arm

c. Imperial garden

6. Nipsey Hussle created which Los Angeles clothing store?

a. Laced

b. The Marathon

c. Up in Bottom

7. Maulana Karenga established which pan African celebration?

a. Santeria

b. Kwanzaa

c. Carnival

8. Lillian Mobley has a center named after her?

a. True

b. False

9. Danny Bakewell created which infamous Los Angeles festival aimed at black business growth?

a. UniverSoul Circus

b. Brotherhood Crusade

c. Taste of Soul

10. Yvonne Wheeler became the first black president of the Communications Workers of American Local 9586 in which year?

a. 1999

b. 1992

c. 1995

GLOSSARY

AFL-CIO: The American Federation of Labor and Congress of Industrial Organizations is the largest federation of unions in the United States. It is made up of fifty-five national and international unions, together representing more than 12 million active and retired workers.

Afflicted: to distress with mental or bodily pain; trouble greatly or grievously

Ascension: astronomy the rising of a star above the horizon

Assassinated: to kill suddenly or secretively, especially a prominent person; murder premeditatedly and treacherously

Black Panthers: A militant Black Power organization founded in the 1960s by Huey Newton and others. Newton proclaimed: "We make the statement, quoting from Chairman Mao, that Political Power comes through the Barrel of a Gun."
Bust: a sculpture of a person's head, shoulders, and chest
Consummate: complete or perfect; supremely skilled; superb
Conceive: to become pregnant.
Cultivating: to develop or improve by education or training; train; refine
Deficiencies: a lack or insufficiency; shortage

Dignitaries: a person who holds a high rank or office, as in the government or church

Empowerment: the giving or delegation of power or authority; authorization

Fundamental: serving as, or being an essential part of, a foundation or basis; basic; underlying

Ideological: the body of doctrine, myth, belief, etc., that guides an individual, social movement, institution, class, or large group

Inhabit: to live or dwell in (a place), as people or animals

Kwanzaa: a harvest festival celebrated from December 26th until January 1st in some African American communities

Mobilize: to marshal, bring together, prepare (power, force, wealth, etc.) for action, especially of a vigorous nature

Radical: thoroughgoing or extreme, especially as regards change from accepted or traditional forms

Reformation: to change to a better state, form, etc.; improve by alteration, substitution, abolition, etc.

Reprimand: a severe reproof or rebuke, especially a formal one by a person in authority

Sharecropper: a tenant farmer who pays as rent a share of the crop

Self-Sufficiency: able to supply one's own or its own needs without external assistance

Sufficient: adequate for the purpose; enough

US Organization, or **Organization Us**: a Black nationalist group in the United States founded in 1965. It was established as a community organization by Hakim Jamal together with Maulana Karenga. It was a rival to the Black Panther Party in California

Vanguard: the forefront in any movement, field, activity, or the like

Watts Riots: A group of violent disturbances in Watts, a largely black section of Los Angeles, in 1965. Over thirty people died in the Watts riots, which were the first of several serious clashes between black people and police in the late 1960s

Welfare: financial or other assistance to an individual or family from a city, state, or national government

www.ingramcontent.com/pod-product-compliance
Lightning Source LLC
Chambersburg PA
CBHW061147010526
44118CB00026B/2895